Simple Mach

What Is a Lever?

By Lloyd G. Douglas

Welcome
Books

Children's Press®
A Division of Scholastic Inc.
New York / Toronto / London / Auckland / Sydney
Mexico City / New Delhi / Hong Kong
Danbury, Connecticut

Photo Credits: Cover and all photos by Maura B. McConnell
Contributing Editor: Jennifer Silate
Book Design: Mindy Liu

Library of Congress Cataloging-in-Publication Data

Douglas, Lloyd G.
What is a lever? / by Lloyd G. Douglas.
   p. cm. -- (Simple machines)
  Includes index.
  Summary: Illustrations and text describe different examples of the use
of simple machines known as levers.
  ISBN 0-516-23963-5 (library binding) -- ISBN 0-516-24022-6 (paperback)
  1. Levers--Juvenile literature. [1. Levers.] I. Title.

TJ147 .D68 2002
621.8'11--dc21

                                       2002001711

Contents

1 Seesaw   8

2 Scissors   12

3 Hammer Claw   16

4 New Words   22

5 To Find Out More   23

6 Index   24

7 About the Author   24

A **lever** is a **simple machine**.

It is used to make work easier.

A lever moves up and down.

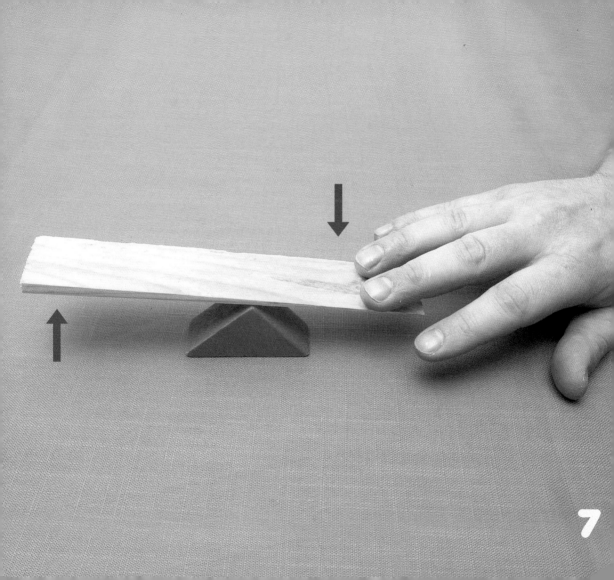

A **seesaw** is a lever.

The seesaw moves up and down on a metal bar.

9

The seesaw helps move people up and down.

The people move easily.

11

Scissors are also levers.

12

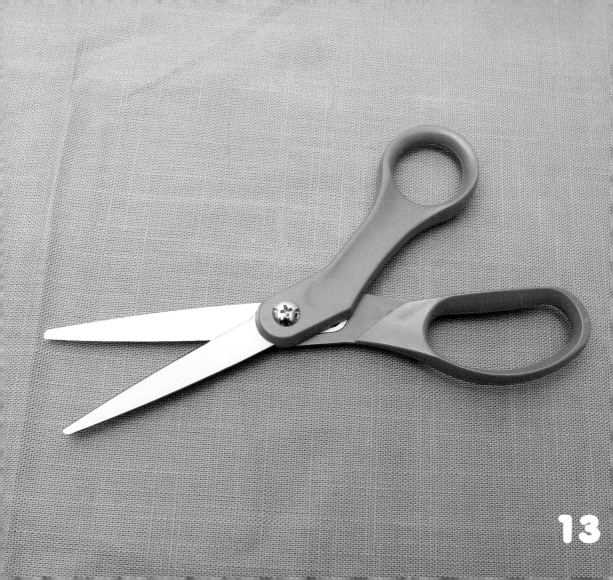

13

The **blades** of the scissors move up and down.

Scissors can cut things easily.

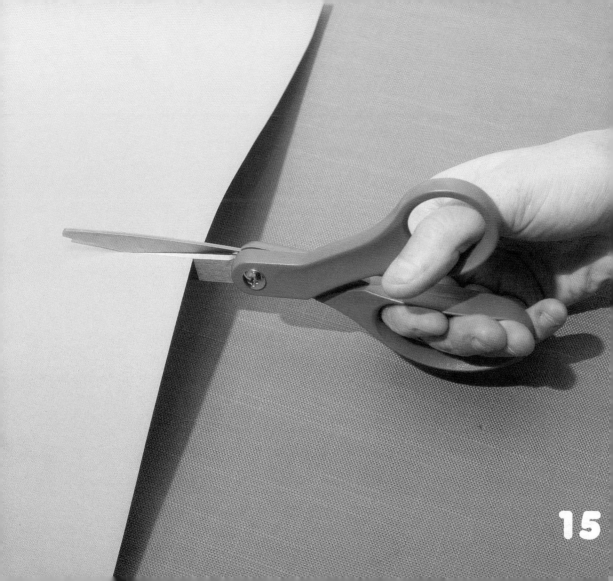

15

A **hammer claw** is also a lever.

16

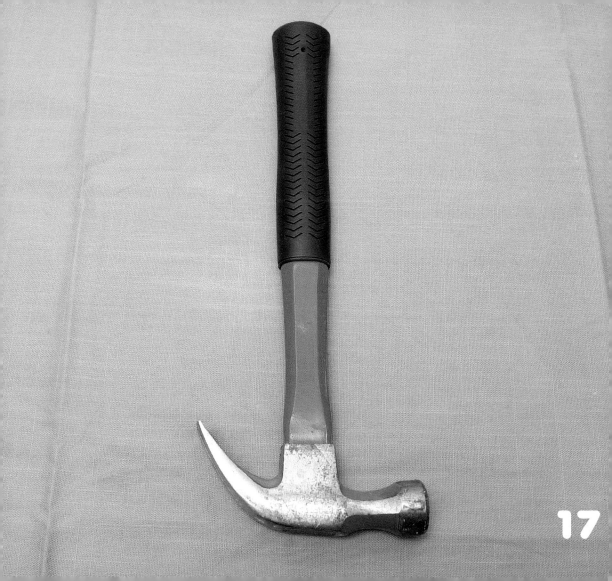

17

The hammer rests on its top.

When the handle is pulled down, the hammer claw goes up.

The hammer claw can take a nail out of wood.

19

Levers can help us do many different things.

They are very helpful simple machines.

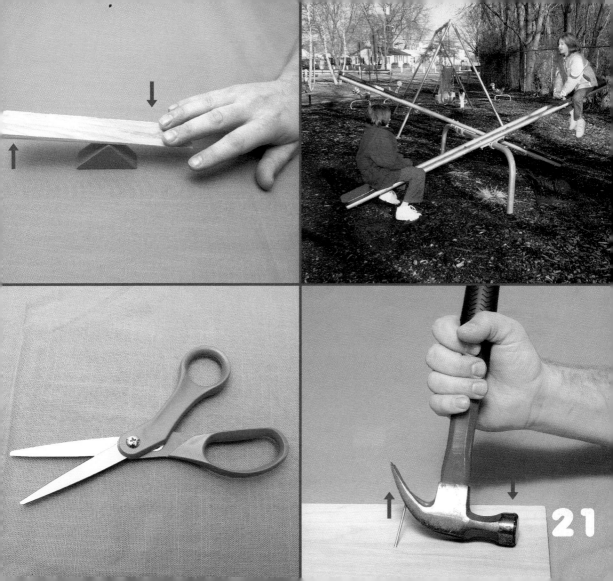

New Words

blades (**blaydz**) the sharp cutting part on scissors

hammer claw (**ham**-ur **klaw**) the top part of a hammer that is used to take nails out of wood

lever (**lev**-ur) a simple machine that moves up and down to make work easier

scissors (**siz**-urz) a sharp tool with two blades used for cutting paper, fabric, and other things

seesaw (**see**-saw) a long board that sits on a support in the middle and goes up and down

simple machine (**sim**-puhl muh-**sheen**) a basic mechanical device that makes work easier

To Find Out More

Books
Levers
by Anne Welsbacher
Capstone Press

The Lever
by Patricia Armentrout
Rourke Press

Web Site
Levers: Simple Machines
http://www.enchantedlearning.com/physics/machines/Levers.shtml
Learn about the different kinds of levers on this informative Web site.

Index

blades, 14

hammer claw, 16, 18

lever, 4, 6, 8, 12, 16, 20

scissors, 12, 14

seesaw, 8, 10

simple machine, 4, 20

About the Author
Lloyd G. Douglas is an editor and writer of children's books.

Reading Consultants
Kris Flynn, Coordinator, Small School District Literacy, The San Diego County Office of Education

Shelly Forys, Certified Reading Recovery Specialist, W.J. Zahnow Elementary School, Waterloo, IL

Sue McAdams, Former President of the North Texas Reading Council of the IRA, and Early Literacy Consultant, Dallas, TX